# Microwave Cooking, The Microwave cookbook Collection

rodney cannon

Published by rodney cannon, 2017.

While every precaution has been taken in the preparation of this book, the publisher assumes no responsibility for errors or omissions, or for damages resulting from the use of the information contained herein.

MICROWAVE COOKING, THE MICROWAVE COOKBOOK COLLECTION

**First edition. April 11, 2017.**

Copyright © 2017 rodney cannon.

Written by rodney cannon.

To my little girl, Delenn. I hope that someday you will out grow TV dinners and french fries.

# MICROWAVE COOKING
# THE MICROWAVE COOK BOOK
# COLLECTION
# COOKING WITH MIC
# &
# DESSERTS WITH MIC
# 30 MICROWAVE DESSERTS

By.
Rodney Cannon

# COOKING WITH MIC

# Chapter One

*"My definition of man is a cooking animal. The beasts have memory, judgment, and the faculties and passions of our minds in a certain degree; but no beast is a cook."* - James Boswell

I have heard it said by many of the world famous chefs that make appearances on the food networks and those who have their own kitchen rescue series on network television that you should never cook with mic, meaning a microwave oven.

Those who earn millions of dollars and have spent decades learning how to become master chefs can say this with a straight face, but to the average person they sounds crazy. Almost every home has a microwave in it and preparing at least a quarter of our meals would be difficult and time consuming without one.

The microwave is a tool like any other. Most of it use it for prepared frozen meals and of course popcorn. Also to reheat takeout meals and left overs. The weakness of the microwave is the act of actually preparing meals from scratch with one. With this book I hope to change that option.

I am not going to give you a massive book that is filled with hundreds of recipes. I have never liked those books. Those books are like walking into a restaurant, sitting down and being handed an eight page menu. Too many choices means too many hard choices.

Should I order this?

Should I pair it with that?

Why does this restaurant have an entire page dedicated to dip?

Who's bright idea was it to divide warm deserts from cold deserts and give them each their own page?

Menus like that and books like that are more than most people can handle so I am going to keep this one relatively short and to the point.

You can cook quality meals with a microwave that do not come from a box in the frozen foods isle.

You can cook quality meals with a microwave from scratch.

Understand that not every recipe will come with a picture. I left some out because I find that pictures can intimidate. If the end result does not look exactly like the picture then it is a failure and nothing could be further from the truth. This is not master chef where you will be judged on appearances. It is about taste and mastering simple recipes. Focus on taste rather than look of the finish product and I promise you that you will be happy.

If you are ready, I have twenty five recipes with a few extras ready for you.

# Chapter Two
# Pizza Crackers

We are going to begin with a short and quick recipe to build your confidence as a master chef.

Our fist cooking with Mic exercise is going to be what are called Pizza Crackers. Do not feel pressure to make it look great. Look does not matter, only taste matters. If you like the taste then you have done a good job.

Now we will gather the basic *ingredients*.

12 – 24 crackers. Any cracker will do. Whole wheat, Ritz, townhouse or saltines.

About ¼ cup of pizza sauce. I would suggest one of the name brand kind for better taste. If it has actual tomato bits in it then even better.

*Toppings.* Slice pepperoni or sausage or what ever you like on top of your pizza even if you are one of those aliens who like pineapple.

½ cup of shredded cheese mozzarella cheese.

A pinch of garlic salt or pizza seasoning for taste.

Now that we have our ingredients we can get around to the fun part, the cooking.

Now you will get a microwave safe plate.

You will evenly space the crackers on the plate.

You will use a teaspoon to evenly coat the center of each cracker.

You will sprinkle cheese on top of sauce. Since this is yours you can go over board with the cheese.

Next add your topping of choice and sprinkle seasoning.

Place in microwave and cook on high for between one to two minutes. You are cooking until the cheese melts. Remove from microwave, cool for a few minutes and enjoy.

Now you have cooked your first meal from scratch with your microwave. Rest and relax. Tomorrow we are going to take a step up.

# Chapter Three
# Thinking Like A Chef

The difference between cooking frozen food straight from a box with a picture on it that never really ends up looking like that picture when it is done and taking the time to do it yourself can be described with one word.

Quality.

You engaging in attention to detail you are creating a meal that is quality.

A home cooked meal has a special appeal because some thought and effort had to be applied before the meal is served. You are going to learn how to do this over time even when cooking with a microwave oven.

You are going to shop for quality ingredients. You are only going to learn what this means over time. With trial and error you will discover what works best in what ever tool that you decide to cook with be it a standard oven, toaster oven or microwave oven.

As you get use to preparing meals for yourself you will grow to love crisp fresh ingredients. You will learn that frozen foods in any form should be the last choice and never the first.

You will discover the best pots and containers to use in your chosen tool. There are a number of containers on the market that will give you the ability to produce amazing food in a microwave and in a future chapter I will introduce you to a few of them.

# Chapter Four
# Mic Can Make Mac And Cheese

I realize that there are dozens of box mixes for one of America's favorite foods, Macaroni and Cheese, but there is nothing like freshly made mac and cheese. So this recipe is going to be one that you will most likely wish to memorize and pull out from time to time and do not worry it does not take long to make it this way.

*Ingredients* that you will need

8 to 10 ounces of macaroni.

3 to 4 tablespoons of salted butter.

1 pound of cubed cheese.

¾ cups of whole milk.

3 table spoons of finely chopped onion.

A pinch of salt and pepper.

In a large microwave dish place the macaroni, add salt and cover with water. Brink water to a boil in the microwave. Check every thirty seconds until you find that the macaroni is al dente then drain and set the macaroni aside.

Next in a 2 quart covered casserole dish heat the butter and chopped onion on high for three to three and a half minutes. Add macaroni, milk and cheese. Stir and then cook in microwave for ten to twelve minutes. You will need to interrupted the cooking every three minutes to stir the mac and cheese. Once you have removed it from the oven it may look runny. Do not worry about this. Season with a little more salt and pepper and then allow it to stand for ten minutes.

Now you are ready to serve. Dig in and enjoy.

You have now learned how to make Mac and Cheese from scratch in a microwave oven. You have two recipes down and twenty nine to go.

# Chapter Five
## Your Best Friends, Salt and Pepper

Perhaps you have watched some of the more popular cooking shows on television and if you have you are familiar with the single biggest complaint that the top chefs make to those who try to impress them with their cooking.

This dish was under seasoned.

There is not enough seasoning on this dish.

In a British accent, "Damn, what a shame if only you had added a little more salt you would be our new master chef."

The message that I am trying to convey is that salt and pepper are your very best friends in the kitchen. It is easy to over do it. Too much salt is the kiss of death and is almost impossible to recover from, but just the right amount of salt can elevate a dish to another level.

The most under salted category of food is meats. People natural assume that most meats have already been salted and do not need any more while it is cooking. Nothing could be further from the truth. Poultry needs salt and pepper to keep it from tasting bland. Do not count on oils or butter to give it flavor. Flavor exist in the meat and salt can bring it to the surface.

Nothing requires the addition of salt more than beef. Salt interacts with beef more so that any other meat. Salt changes the texture of beef. It alters the moisture levels of the meat and enhances the natural flavor. Do not be afraid to experiment with salting meat before cooking. I know that there has been decades of propaganda about how bad salt is for you. You need to dismiss this when it comes to cooking. Salt is need in the same way that a car needs gasoline. Yes there are cars that can go without gas, but the fastest and the best still run on it. The same can be said for meals.

# Chapter Six
## Stir Fry Time

This recipe has more layers than you would think so give yourself at least forty minutes to do this the first time around. As you master a recipe the prep time will degrees.

First thing that you are going to have to do is to boil some rice. I would suggest no more than half a cup. For those of you who have never gone beyond the rice in a bag stage a little dry rice makes a great deal of cooked rice. You do not want to dump a five pound bag in a pot of boiling water. You will end up with something that resembles a missing episode from I Love Lucy.

Once the rice has been prepared set it aside and get ready to cook with our good friend Mic.

*Ingredients*

¼ cup of flour

1table spoon of salt

¼ teaspoon of ground or powdered cumin

¼ teaspoon of ground pepper

about 1 pound of steak that has been cut into thin strips. I recommend sirloin steak, but you can use other cuts.

1 tablespoons vegetable oil.

1 13 to 15 ounce can of diced tomatoes.

2 to 3 carrots sliced into thin strips. A chef would say that you will need to julienne your carrots, but ever time I hear that word I think of The Sound of Music.

½ cups of diced onion.

½ teaspoon of dried basil

½ teaspoon of oregano

1 cup of thinly stripped zucchini.

1 and ½ cups of sliced mushrooms.

1 ziplock bag.

You will now combine the first four ingredients into the bag and then you will add the meat before resealing. Shake bag until meat is coated.

Pour oil into 2 quart size microwave dish and space meat evenly. Cover dish, place inside over and set oven at 50 percent.

Cook for about 6 minutes. Stir at least once while cooking. Now you will set this aside.

Drain liquid from tomatoes into a cup before placing tomatoes into a bowl. Now combine liquid from tomatoes into a bowl with oregano,carrots, onions and basil. Cover bowl and microwave on high for 4 minutes.

Pour over meat and now you will add the tomatoes, zucchini and mushrooms. Cover dish and cook at 50 percent power for 12 minutes. This is called stir fry for a reason. So now you are going to stir this every two minutes until cooking time ends.

Serve over rice and you have just completed another recipe.

Give yourself a pat on the back and mark this date on the calendar. The day that you mastered stir frying with your best friend Mic.

# Chapter Seven
## Salsa Time

We are now going to do something easy next. We are going to make Salsa. This recipe can be completed in less than ten minutes and the actual cooking time is less than one minute.

*Ingredients*

Three chopped tomatoes.

1 small sliced onion.

1 minced clove of garlic.

3 tablespoons of chopped green pepper.

1 tablespoons lemon juice.

1 ½ teaspoons minced basil

½ teaspoon chili powder

1 teaspoon salt

½ teaspoon pepper

1 bag of tortilla chips.

Grab your microwave safe bowl and combine the tomatoes, onions and garlic, stir. Then you will add the green pepper, lemon juice and the rest of the ingredients. Mix well. Now you will microwave on high for one minute.

Now grab your chips and kick back, you have made salsa.

# Chapter Eight
# Chicken Teriyaki

Ingredients, yes I am going straight to ingredients this chapter. I am hungry and I want to get to it.

*Ingredients*

¼ cup soy sauce.

2 tablespoons ketchup.

2 tablespoons garlic powder.

3 tablespoons sugar.

1 boneless chicken breast cut into strips.

Mix soy sauce, ketchup, garlic powder and sugar in a bowl. Drop chicken into bowl and toss until coated. Now place chicken on microwave plate. Cover chicken with plastic wrap and place in microwave oven. Cook on high for 6 to 8 minutes until chicken is no longer pink inside and you are done.

There now wasn't that recipe easy to handle. When you heard chicken Teriyaki I bet that you were tempted to skip this chapter and now that it is done you cannot wait to cook it again.

# Chapter Nine
# Bacon

There are rumors that you cannot make bacon in a microwave oven. Nothing could be further from the truth. Mic can cook bacon. Will it be soggy or crispy?

Good question.

Mic is your friend. Would a friend give you soggy bacon? No, of course not. Mic will give you nice and crisp slices of bacon.

This is how you are going to make bacon in a microwave. You will need only three things.

A microwave safe plate.

A few paper towels. Do not get the cheap ones. This is bacon my friend. Breakfast is the most important meal of the day. You are going to have to spend more than 69 cents a roll.

Bacon. Buy some real bacon. I am not sure if this works with beef or turkey bacon.

Now you will lay the a paper towel on a microwave safe plate. Next lay 2 strips of bacon on the paper towel. Fold the towel over to cover the bacon and cook on high for one and a half to two minutes. Remove from over and you will find a greasy mound of paper towel. This does not matter. You are not going to eat the paper towels you are going to be eating the bacon. Remove bacon strips from paper towel and you will find perfectly crisp bacon. Next, if I have to encourage you to eat bacon there is something wrong here.

# Chapter Ten
# Scrambled Eggs

What is bacon without eggs.

You can boil and egg with a microwave. You can poach an egg with a microwave, but I like my eggs scrambled. Scrambled eggs and bacon, bacon and more bacon.

It is really not that hard to scramble an egg in the microwave oven once you think about it for a while.

*Ingredients*

2 eggs, if you want more you will need to adjust the other ingredients.

2 tablespoons of milk.

1 tablespoon of shredded cheese.

½ teaspoon of salt and pepper.

Cooking spray or oil.

Coat pan with cooking spray. Add eggs and milk. Beat them together and now you are going to microwave on high for 45 seconds. Stir the eggs while adding salt and pepper then give them another thirty seconds or until they are set. Add cheese to top for flavor and your scrambled eggs are done.

You could at this point dig into those eggs or you could add some more bacon. That is what I would do.

# Chapter Eleven
## What About Vegetarians

*"Vegetarians, and their Hezbollah-like splinter faction, the vegans ... are the enemy of everything good and decent in the human spirit."*
— Anthony Bourdain

What about the Vegetarians? Shouldn't I have a few chapters dedicated to them?

My answer is no.

They can go eat raw food. Is there no tofu, no organically grown walnuts (if it grows on a tree it is organic by definition) or aged tree bark. In other words I do not know how to cook a banana in a microwave. They tend to explode.

I believe that the microwave was invented by a carnavour who was in a hurry to consume more meat. Tasty and fresh from behind taken out by a hunter armed with one of those kind of guns that robocop carries.

The microwave was invented during a time when rock and roll ruled the earth and Grace Kelly was on the cover of every magazine and Law and Order was finish up its first season on television. In other words including vegetarian meals in a book about cooking with Mic seems UN - American.

If that does not make clear my feelings on this subject then perhaps one magic word will.

Bacon.

# Chapter Twelve
## Taco Time

Who does not love a good taco. They come in some many forms and flavors. There are fish tacos and chicken, pork and my favorite beef tacos. We have the hard shell and the soft shell kind.

The thing that you may no know from the eater's side of things is that no only are they fun to eat they are fun to make.

This is one of those top three recipes that you are going to want to remember. If you are ready here we go again.

*Ingredients*
1 pound ground beef
1 ½ teaspoons chili powder
1 teaspoon salt
½ teaspoon garlic powder
1/8 teaspoon cayenne pepper
¼ cup water
box or pack of taco shells,
2 cups shredded taco cheese
2 cups shredded lettuce
¼ cup chopped onion
1 chopped tomato,
taco sauce in a jar or can

Now you will crumble beef into a microwave safe pan or dish with lid. Put lid in place and cook on high for 5 full minutes.

Drain pan of fluid. Now you will stir in the chili powder, garlic powder, salt and pepper. Then you will add the water and stir again.

Cover pan and return to microwave where you will cook for another 3 and a half to 4 minutes.

Next give the shells a quick zap in the oven, 30 seconds should do. Now comes the fun part. You are ready to build your taco. To each shell add 2 to 3 tablespoons of beef and then add your toppings of lettuce, tomato,onion, cheese and of course the sauce.

You can substitute the ground beef in this recipe with any other ground meat. The adjustments that I would make is to cook ground pork a little longer and ground chicken not as long because chicken with become tough if over cooked in a microwave.

# Chapter Thirteen
## Cooking With Attitude

*"The only real stumbling block is fear of failure. In cooking you've got to have a what-the-hell attitude."* - Julia Child

Anyone can make toast, well anyone, but my ex. There is no one who goes into a panic when toast is mentioned, but mention what appears to be a complex recipe then that is where the fear begins to set in.

You are not learning how to fly a fighter jet and lives are not at stake. Your microwave oven will survive all of your efforts to master the recipes in this book as long as you remember not to leave a fork or a spoon inside it.

With is book I have tried to build your confidence slowly, recipe by recipe. I know that any of your are have skipped some or are planning to skip over a few recipes that sound too hard or have too many ingredients.

You are doing that ingredient glance aren't you? More than ten ingredients and you move on to the next even if it is something you really like to eat.

Put away your fears of failure. You will fail from time to time no matter what you attempt. We learn more from our failures that from success. You will under cook or over cook some of these recipes and true failure only happens when you quit and do not try again.

The goal when learning how to do something new is not to ever fail, but to pick up the pieces, to examine them and to try again and again until you get it right. The world admires the can do kind of people. Let me clue you in on something that all the can doers learn as they go along. Can do becomes will do. I will do whatever I set my mind to do. I am able to say this because three years and six books ago I was a can doer. I can write a book I know I can was my mindset each and every day. There were days of doubt and times when I actually allowed myself to quit only to pick myself up and get back to work a few hours later.

You are reading this book because I failed more times than I will ever admit to. I believe that if you have read this far then you will reach the end of this road with a brand new skill set. You will not be a master chef, but you will be able to cook a month worth of meals.

# Chapter Fourteen
## Risotto

For all of us who have spent the last decade or so watching television's most popular chef know know that this is nothing he cares about more than how this particular dish is cooked. Chef Ramsey has spent more time on Hell's Kitchen scream about and sending this dish back to be redone than all other dishes combined.Bloody hell, it is Risotto.

It is rice. Sounds easy when you say it like that, but the truth is that it can be done any number of ways and because of this it can fail in so many ways. Do not let that bother you or intimidate you. If it does not turn out perfectly the first time no one is going to yell at you, slam you dish down and insult everyone that you have ever known all the way back to your seventh grade home room teacher.

I promise that you can do this and you will be shocked at how easy it really is.

So are your ready to make Risotto?

What do you mean no?

I will not take no for an answer. You are going to make risotto. Now go grab these ingredients and lets get to work.

*Ingredients*

3 cups hot chicken broth

1/2 teaspoon salt

1//2 teaspoon ground white or black pepper

2 tablespoons butter

2 tablespoons olive oil

1/2 cup minced yellow onion

1 cup uncooked medium grain white rice

¼ cup freshly grated Parmesan cheese

First the chick broth you do not have to make, you can get it in a can. It can be found in most supermarkets near the can soup.

Now you will combine the broth with the salt and pepper into a pan and you will warm this over a burner. You could do this in the microwave, but you are going to be needing the microwave oven for other things. So warm the broth mix on the burner and once it has gotten hot, turn it to the lowest possible simmer and move on to next step.

In a dish you are going to place the butter and olive oil. Next you will heat it in the microwave for 2 minutes. Next you will add the onions to the dish and then you will stir until coated. Now cook this for 4 minutes. Add the rice, stir and then cook for another 4 minutes.

Now you will pour the chicken broth mix over the rice and you are going to give it all a good stirring. Place back in microwave oven and cook for 9 minutes. Stir it good and cook for another 9 minutes, making this part of the cooking a total of 18 minutes.

The moment that you remove it from the microwave over you must stir in the Parmesan cheese.

Now plate it and serve. Remember plating is important. We do not want the Risotto to be sent back to the kitchen. We do not want to get yelled at do we?

What?

You cooked this for yourself.

Blood hell then, you can forget the plating. Just grab a fork or a cooking spoon or even your fingers and dig right in.

You have just finished a Risotto that is good enough for anyone, but a English chef who cannot keep his shirt on for an entire episode of his show.

# Chapter Fifteen
## Pacing Yourself

As I near the halfway point of this book I thought that I would take time to suggest that you takes some time as well.

Just because this book is designed to offer up thirty one recipes for a thirty one day month this does not mean that you have to do them all back to back. You are not only allowed, but you are now being encouraged to take a break or two along the way.

You do not have to face the microwave challenge everyday. You are allowed to use the stove top or even the actual oven. You can even go out to dinner. Cold cuts are encouraged. You can even order yourself a pizza.

Look at this as you would weight training. You are not suppose to work the same muscles everyday. You have to mix it up to see gain maximum impact from the work that you are doing.

There is one rule that must be maintained while taking time away from learning and mastering these recipes. You are not allowed to revert to throwing boxes of frozen food into Mic. He only cooks meals that you have prepared until you have mastered these recipes. That is the deal you must accept before taking time away.

Now if your batteries are fully recharged it is time to get back to cooking with Mic.

# Chapter Sixteen
# Corn on the Cob

This is a really simple one.

It is my way of getting you back on the horse after your insanely long break from this book.

If you are ready I would suggest that you will need to check your savings account and your credit card limit. You have to purchase the needed ingredients for this one.

*Ingredients*

1 ear of corn.

Paper towels.

1 stick of butter.

I hope that you did not have difficulty carrying that back from the store and that you did not have to make two trips or pay extra to have these many ingredients delivered.

You will now remove the husk from the ear of corn. Wrap the ear of corn in a moist paper towel. By moist I mean that it should drip water if you were to hold it out before you. Now wrap the corn in the towel and place it on a microwave safe plate. Place in over and cook on high for 5 minutes. Remove paper towel and you know what to do with the butter.

You can also cook it by placing corn in a dish, filling dish with water until corn floats. Covering dish and boiling it in oven for 5 minutes.

# Chapter Seventeen
# Red Snapper

*"I read recipes the same way I read science fiction. I get to the end and say to myself "well, that's not going to happen"* - Rita Rudner
Now we are going to tackle red snapper. You can purchase this already filleted or do it yourself. I would suggest buying it pre – cut and ready to prepare.

*Ingredients*
4 fillets red snapper
¾ cup sour cream
¼ cup mayonnaise
3 tablespoons milk
1 tablespoon prepared mustard
1 ½ teaspoons dill weed
cooked rice

If red snapper has not been cut into serving sized pieces you will have to do so now. Next place in a microwave safe dish. Cover and cook for 4 minutes. Drain dish.

Next you will combine sour cream, mayonnaise, mustard and milk and dill. Mix well. Now coat fish with half of the mix. Return to microwave and cook on high for another 4 minutes.

Quickly cook rice while fish is cooking and serve fish with rice and what remains of the mix.

Fish is not as easy as you would think and I had to attempt this recipe more than twice before I was happy with the results. Adjust the cooking time of fish depending upon size to get best results.

# Chapter Eighteen
## Swiss Steak

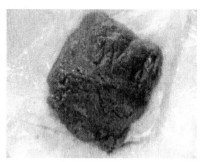

*"Cooking is not a science but an art, mistakes are okay, messes are fine, the pleasure is in the creating and the sharing of the result."* -
Lori Pollan

Today we are going to be making Swiss Steak.

*Ingredients*

1 ½ pounds boneless round steak (¼ inch thick)

3tablespoons onion soup mix

1 (4 ounce) can mushroom stems and pieces, drained

1 (14.5 ounce) can diced tomatoes

2 tablespoons cornstarch

¼ teaspoon pepper

1 dash cayenne pepper

1 teaspoon salt

Cut steak in to serving sized pieces and then you are going to pound the steak with a mallet until tender or it can no longer continue to fight. Next place steak on a microwave safe pan and sprinkle with mushrooms and soup mix. Drain your can of tomatoes, be sure to save the fluid in a bowl. Set aside the tomatoes and now combine cornstarch with fluid. Add pepper, cayenne pepper, salt and tomatoes. Mix and pour over steak.

Cover and microwave on high for 6 to 7 minutes. Once it has begun to boil you will turn microwave down to 50% power and cook for 22 – 25 minutes or until meat is tender.

You have just finished another recipe.

# Chapter Nineteen
## The Lazy Myth

I realize that there is a myth that those who cook with a microwave oven do so because they are lazy. I have always thought that I love cooking with Mic because I love to be efficient. The ability to set a timer and know that when you hear that lovely beeping sound the meal is ready is a miracle of modern science.

People who use a toaster or a pressure cooker are not considered lazy. The lazy ones are those human turtles who cook with crock pots. Put the food in crock pot and comeback ten hours later to see if it is warm and I am talking about soup.

So the first thing that you must overcome as you become a microwave chef is the feeling that what you are doing is not as difficult as any other kind of cooking. Think about the journey that you have taken so far. It has at times been fun, but it has also required effort. If you were lazy you would have stuck to TV dinners. You are doing hard work and engaging in a journey that is giving you a brand new skill set that will be with you for a lifetime or until they invent androids that will do all the cooking for us or better still terminators. Yes terminators who cook using blow torches and powerful explosives to cook meat.

Until then we are going to be forced to do it this way.

Are you ready to get back to the cooking? I have to warn you that it is going to get a little more difficult.

# Chapter Twenty
# Clam Chowder

You can make your clam chowder look as lovely as you wish. I am one of those people who loves the look of clam chowder while not loving the taste of it. I am more of a chicken noodle soup guy. But then again there is the absolute best thing about clam chowder.

Saying clam chowder in a think New England accent. You know like the doctor on Murder She Wrote. "Would you like a bowl of clam chowder Jessica? Forget the fact that more people get murdered in Cabot Cove than Detroit, let's all looked shocked every time we find a body and talk about it over a nice bowl of clam chowder."

Now are we ready to make some clam chowder?

Cool. This is where we start.

*Ingredients*

4 slices bacon, cut into ½ inch pieces

2 (6.5 ounce) cans chopped clams

1 ½ cups diced peeled raw potatoes

1/3 cup chopped onion

2 tablespoons all-purpose flour
1 ½ cups milk, divided
½ teaspoon salt
1 pinch pepper
1 teaspoon butter or margarine
Minced fresh parsley

We need a two quart size microwave dish. Now cook bacon on high for 4 to 5 minutes. Remove bacon from dish and set aside.

Next you are going to drain clam juice into the pan. Mix in potatoes and onions. Cover and cook for 9 to ten minutes on high. You will want to interrupt cooking at least once to give it a good stirring. Now you will mix the flour with ¼ cup of milk. Stir into mixture. Next you will add salt and pepper with the rest of the milk.

Now you will cover it and cook at 50% for 6 – 7 minutes. Stir at least twice while cooking. Rest for a 2 minutes. Now stir in clams and butter. Rest for another 2 minutes and now you can garnish with bacon and parsley. You have just made a clam chowder.

You will want to experiment with cooking times a little to get this recipe just right for you.

# Chapter Twenty One
# Fried Rice

This recipe for microwave fried rice is going to be a quick and easy one to do. You may notice that there is no salt in the recipe, this is because there is a good deal of salt in soy sauce and bouillon and of course ham.

*Ingredients*
1 tablespoon vegetable oil
½ cup sliced green onions
1 medium carrot, shredded
1 garlic clove, minced
2 cups water
1 cup uncooked long grain rice
1 tablespoon beef or chicken bouillon granules
¾ cup Frozen Peas, thawed
2 tablespoons soy sauce
1 ¼ cups chopped cooked ham
2 eggs

Grab a two quart microwave safe dish. In it you will combine the oil, carrot, garlic and onions. Cover and cook for 3 - 4 minutes. Now mix in water, rice and bouillon. Cover and cook on high for 14 – 18 minutes. Now stir in peas, soy sauce and ham. Cover and let rest for five minutes.

Now in a microwave safe bowl you will beat the eggs. Next cover and cook on high for about 1 ½ minutes or until eggs are firm.

Dice egg and stir into the rice. You are now ready to serve.

# Chapter Twenty Two
## Microwave Goulash

The word Goulash sounds funny and sloppy. It sounds like something a barbarian would love to dig into. Goulash and a mug of ale or meed. It is really the same thing, but it sounds more hardcore when you say meed.

Let's make some goulash and wash it down with some meed or diet cola.

*Ingredients*
1 (8 ounce) package uncooked elbow macaroni
1 pound ground beef
1 cup diced onion
1 cup sliced celery
1 tablespoon minced garlic
1 (14.5 ounce) can diced tomatoes
1 (10 ounce) can tomato sauce
1 tablespoon sugar
1 tablespoon paprika
1 teaspoon dried oregano
¼ teaspoon caraway seed
1 pinch cayenne pepper, or to taste
1 teaspoon salt

You will bring a quart of water to a boil, add salt and then the macaroni to water. Cook for 6 to 8 minutes or until tender then drain.

At the same time you crumble the beef into a 2 quart dish. Add the onions, celery and garlic. Cook at high for about 6 minutes.

Stir once or twice while cooking and drain when done.

Next stir Tomatoes, sugar and tomato sauce into beef. Add paprika, oregano and caraway seeds, salt and cayenne pepper. Cover and cook for 9 to 14 minutes. When celery is tender it is done.

Remove from over, stir in macaroni and cook for 3 more minutes.

You are now done and ready to serve.

# Chapter Twenty Three
## French Toast

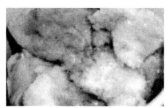

*"I was seven before I realized that you could eat breakfast with your pants on."* Christopher Moore

It may actually be faster to make french toast in a microwave than the standard way.

*Ingredients*

2 slices of bread, any kind

1/8 stick of butter

½ teaspoon of cinnamon

3 tablespoons of milk

¼ teaspoon vanilla exact

1 egg

First cut your bread into small squares. Now grab a mug and you are going to coat the inside with the butter. Place bread inside of mug.

Now in a second mug or bowl you are going to mix the egg, milk, cinnamon and vanilla with a fork. When mixed fully you will pour over bread.

Now allow bread to soak in the mixture for a minute before placing mug in microwave oven. Cook on high for 2 minutes and you are ready to let the syrup flow and eat.

# Chapter Twenty Four
# Fettuccine Alfredo

*Ingredients*

2 ounces uncooked fettuccine

3 tablespoons half-and-half cream

1 ounce cream cheese, cubed

3 tablespoons shredded

Parmesan cheese

1/8 teaspoon salt

1/8 teaspoon white pepper

Now you will bring a pot of water to a boil and then you will cook the fettuccine for 7 – 10 minutes or until al dente.

While fettuccine is cooking you will combine cream and cream cheese in a microwave safe bowl. Cook at 50% power for 2 to 2 and a half minutes. Remove from oven and stir in Parmesan cheese until creamy. Lastly you can add the salt and pepper.

Drain the fettuccine and stir into sauce.

You have now learned how to make fettuccine Alfredo in a microwave.

# Chapter Twenty Five
# Baked Potato

There is not that much difference between baking a potato in an actual oven and a microwave oven. Which means that the taste is going to be almost identical.

*Ingredients*

1 large russet potato

1 tablespoon butter or margarine

3 tablespoons shredded Cheddar cheese

salt and pepper to taste

3 teaspoons sour cream

Scrub the potato. Try to do this lightly, do not scrub the potato as if it is about to perform surgery. Next you will prick the potato a few times with a fork. No more than a half an inch deep.

Next you will place it one a microwave safe plate and cook at full power for 5 minutes. Now turn it over once and cook for another 5 minutes.

When the potato has softened you will remove it from oven and cut it down the center length wise. Now you will season with salt and pepper and mash up the inside with your fork. Now top with butter and 2 tablespoons of cheese.

Cook for one more minute in the microwave oven. Remove and top with 1 tablespoon of cheese and the sour cream.

Your baked potato is done and you are ready to dig in.

# Chapter Twenty Six
## Chili Time

Chili is one of those universal foods that is made all over America and with every type of meat imaginable. From Alligator to ostrich to rattle snake. I do not recommend those meats for your first try. Let's keep it simple and tradition today with a beef chili.

*Ingredients*

1 pound ground beef

1 medium onion, finely chopped

2 (14.5 ounce) cans stewed tomatoes

2 teaspoons chili powder

1 ½ teaspoons prepared mustard

1 (16 ounce) can kidney beans, rinsed and drained

salt and pepper to taste

Put beef in a microwave safe 2 quart size bowl. Add the onions and mix well.

Cover and cook on high for 5 minutes. Next you will drain and at the tomatoes, mustard and chili powder. Mix well, cover and cook on high for 10 minutes. Now you will add beans and mix before cooking another 3 minutes on high. Add the salt and pepper and you are ready to eat some chili.

# Chapter Twenty Seven
## Microwaving a Chicken

*"In Louisiana, one of the first stages of grief is eating your weight in Popeyes fried chicken. The second stage is doing the same with boudin. People have been known to swap the order. Or to do both at the same time."* - Ken Wheaton

Chicken is the number one protein in the country and I cook it in one form or another at least three days each week.

*Ingredients*

One 3 – 4 pound chicken

½ teaspoons of pepper

¼ teaspoon sage

¼ teaspoon rosemary

¼ teaspoon onion salt

1 tablespoon Kosher salt

1 onion cut into quarters

¼ stick of butter

First find your sharpest kitchen knife and with it you are going to carefully remove the skin from the chicken. Now you will place the chicken on a microwave safe pane. Next you are going to mix together all of the spices and rub down your bird. Now put the onion inside the chicken. Now set your microwave at 50% and cook for thirty minutes. Check the bird and set your oven up to high and cook for another 7 to 10 minutes.

Pull from oven, rub butter on the chicken and set the chicken aside to rest for about ten minutes. It should smell great and taste even better. Cut chicken and enjoy.

# Chapter Twenty Eight
## Curried Chicken

Do not panic or be afraid. Curry in any form is not that hard to make. If it was it would not be so popular. You can and will master this recipe after one or two tries. If you are ready we can get started.

*Ingredients*
1 apple – peeled, cored, and chopped
1 onion, chopped
2 tablespoons butter
3 teaspoons curry powder
1 (10.75 ounce) can condensed cream of mushroom soup
1 cup heavy cream
salt and pepper to taste
8 chicken thighs, cut into bite size pieces
¾ cup fresh sliced mushrooms
1 teaspoon paprika

In a dish you are going to mix the apples and onions with the curry powder and butter. Now you will microwave on high for 3 minutes. Next you will add the cream, salt and pepper along with the can of soup.

Now you will place the chicken in a dish and pour the curry mix over it. Top with the paprika. Next cover with wax paper and microwave at full for 30 minutes. Test to see if chicken is tender. If not give it another two minutes.

Your curried chicken is ready.

# Chapter Twenty Nine
## Parchment Paper

Parchment paper is not just for baking cookies. This great item is the perfect thing to use when cooking fish in a microwave oven.

In a standard oven you can cook fish in a paper bag, but this is not easily done in a microwave. Using parchment paper as a substitute is the perfect solution. Some have made the argument that fish taste better when cooked this way in a microwave rather than the paper bag in a standard oven.

# Chapter Thirty
## Salmon in a Bag

This is fish en papillote or for those of us who do not like fancy names for simple things, it is fish in a bag or in this case in parchment paper. This is amazingly easy to do and after you have tried this recipe I am pretty sure that you will begin to create variation of it with other types of fish.

*Ingredients*

1 square of parchment paper 12 – 14 inches
1 red potato
1 thinly sliced salmon fillet
¼ teaspoon salt
A dash of pepper
1 teaspoon of white wine

You are now going to season the fish with salt and pepper. Next you will thinly slice the potato and uses these slices to form a bed onto of the parchment paper.

Next you will place fish on top of potatoes. Now sprinkle wine over fish. Next you will fold paper over fish as tight as possible to form a bag like container and now you are going to place this on a plate and put it into the microwave oven. Cook for 3 ½ to 4 minutes on high.

Remove from oven. Open parchment paper and you are ready to eat.

# Chapter Thirty One
# Meatball Sandwich Time

I love meatball sandwiches. Being from the home of both the cheese steak and the hoagie I am use to eating them on the best sandwich rolls on earth so that makes me a little prejudice toward them.

You can get by using what ever kind of roll that you wish as long as you do not use hot dog or hamburger rolls. That would just be plain wrong. You need a heartier roll to stuff with meatball goodness.

The recipe that I am going to introduce to you today suggest frozen meatball. If you know how to I would take the time to make home made meatballs. Secondly you are going to get a jar of spaghetti sauce. I could say that any sauce will do, but I have made dozens of meatball sandwiches (okay hundreds) and I have tried different types of sauces. I find that basic Ragu sauce is the best for this job. I wish that I was being paid to say that, but it is just my humble opinion.

*Ingredients*
10 slices provolone cheese
1 (14 ounce) package frozen cooked meatballs
1 (28 ounce) jar spaghetti sauce
5 hoagie rolls, split lengthwise

Put the meatballs into a dish and warm them for 30 to 45 seconds on high. Next you will cover the meatballs with the spaghetti sauce. Cover and cook on high for about 3 minute. Remove from oven.

Slice your rolls and now you can either add the cheese to the rolls before adding the meatballs. Some people like them plan.

Once cheese has been added place meatballs on top and then top meatballs with more cheese. Yeah, you heard me, more cheese. Next pop them back in the oven for 30 seconds to melt the cheese and your meatball sandwich are ready.

# Chapter Thirty Two
## Frittata

Say it, *frittata*.

Now say it again, *frittata*.

I just love the way that sounds.

*Ingredients*

1 tablespoon butter

1 cup cubed fully cooked ham

½ cup chopped onion

¼ cup chopped green pepper

4 egg, beaten

salt and pepper to taste

Place butter on microwave dish put in oven for 20 to 30 seconds or until butter is melted. Now add onions, ham, green pepper, cover and cook on high for 2 minutes.

Next stir in eggs, salt and pepper. Now cook on high for 2 to 2 ½ minutes. Remove from oven. Let stand for 3 minutes or until completely set then cut into wedges.

# Chapter Thirty Three
# Corn Chowder

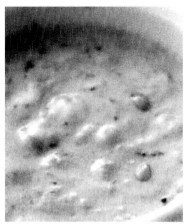

What can I say about corn chowder except that it is like clam chowder only with corn.

*Ingredients*

2 cups water

2 cups diced peeled potatoes

½ cup sliced carrots

½ cup sliced celery

¼ cup chopped onion

1 teaspoon salt

¼ teaspoon pepper

¼ cup butter or margarine

¼ cup all-purpose flour

2 cups milk

3 cups shredded Cheddar cheese

2 (14.75 ounce) cans cream-style corn

Grab two quart size dish and pour the water into it. Put it in the oven and bring to a boil, 5 – 8 minutes on high. Now add the carrots, celery, onions, pepper and the salt. Now you will cook this uncovered for about ten minutes. Now set this aside.

In a second dish you are going to first melt the butter, 45 – 60 seconds will do. Now stir in the flour and then add in the milk slowly. Next you will cook, uncovered, for 6 – 7 minutes, while stirring every few minutes. Now add in the cheese and cook for another 90 seconds.

Now you can stir in both cans of corn and then the vegetable mix that you prepared earlier. Cook on high for about three minutes and you are done.

# Chapter Thirty Four
## Desserts

Dessert is probably the most important stage of the mean, since it will be the last thing your guests remember before they pass out all over the table. - William Powell

I had mixed emotions about including any deserts in this book because I am doing a second book that features nothing but microwave desserts. In the end the only reason that I could come up with to leave desserts off the list of recipes is the quest for more money.

If I write the very best book that I can this time and the best book next time then the money will find me. So here it comes. I am going to close this book with a pair of super sweet and tasty desserts.

The first up is going to be chocolate cake. There are a number of desserts that I could have jumped into, but let's face it there is just nothing that can compete with chocolate in all of its forms.

# Chapter Thirty Five
# Microwave Chocolate Cake

*"Strength is the capacity to break a Hershey bar into four pieces with your bare hands - and then eat just one of the pieces."* - Judith Viorst

I feel sorry that Shakespeare did not write volumes about the joy of chocolate. If I could go back in time I would drop him an m&m gift box. Chocolate is one of those rare universe items that goes with almost everything. Chocolate is like the tasty version of mash potatoes.

We are going to be making a chocolate cake in our microwave today. I love chocolate cake and to be perfectly honest the microwave would be my third choice for dealing with chocolate cake. My first choice would be to eat the cake batter and wash it down with some hersey's syrup. The second choice would be a standard oven because cake makes better in a normal over. All of that said I am ready to do this with the microwave. Just remember that at any time you can stop and eat the batter with your hands. You will not be breaking any rules if you just pretend to pass out so that you can plant your face in the bowl and have to eat your way out.

*Ingredients*
3 tablespoons butter, softened
¼ cup white sugar
1 egg
1 teaspoon vanilla extract
¼ cup milk
½ cup all-purpose flour
2 tablespoons cocoa powder
¼ teaspoon baking powder and 1 pinch salt

Find a microwave safe pan and coat it with non-stick spray before setting it aside. Next you are going to grab a mixing bowl and mix the butter, eggs, vanilla extract and mix. Mix this well before adding salt, flour, cocoa powder and baking powder. Now you must blend this mixture until it is smooth.

Pour into pan and cook for 2 and ½ minutes to 3 minutes. It is done with cake springs back when pressed. Now you will allow the cake to rest for five minutes before finding a plate. You will now place the plate onto of the dish with the open face of the plate down. You will flip dish and cake should fall onto plate with no problem. You have just made a chocolate cake. You can now sit down to eat.

Oh, I almost forgot. Icing. I would suggest chocolate icing with maybe chocolate chips or better yet fudge.

# Chapter Thirty Six
# Oh Fudge

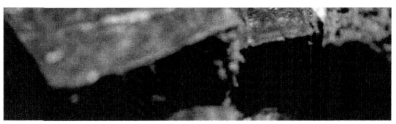

There is a difference between fudge and chocolate cake. The major one is that you have to try harder to chew fudge. Also you may want to include something cool and tasty to wash that delicious fudge down with.

This is a short recipe that is simple to pull off.

*Ingredients*

4 cups confectioners' sugar
½ cup unsweetened cocoa
powder
¼ cup milk
½ cup butter
2 teaspoons vanilla extract

Spray some non-stick on a microwave safe pan and set it aside.

Next in a bowl you are going to mix the confectioners sugar and the cocoa powder. Now pour milk over mixture and drop butter on top. Do not mix. You are going to place this in the oven and cook for 2 minutes. Next you are going to stir in the vanilla until mix is smooth.

Next you will pour into prepared dish and you are going to place this in the freezer for ten minutes. It will thicken and firm up in the freeze. You can now take it out, cut into squares and eat.

# Chapter Thirty Seven
# A Microwave Chef is Born

You have gone through basic training. You have fought the wars. You have made friends with some recipes and enemies of others.

I would like to say that I am proud of you. Job well done. There is nothing like completing a cook book. You are now a hero to the millions and millions who could not do it. Those who quit along the way or were roasted by dragons or consumed by white walkers during the long winter. Sure mastering a few cook books will never put you on the iron throne, but it may some day lead to iron chef or joining a fight club with Bobby Flay.

# DESSERTS WITH MIC
# 30 MICROWAVE DESSERTS

# Chapter One

*"Dessert is to a meal what a dress is to a woman."* - Beatrice Peltr
I wish to first thank those of you who read my book Cooking with Mic and decided to continue your microwave education.

The microwave has long been looked upon as a glorified toaster by those who use them. It is good for popcorn and hot pockets and TV dinners, but making actual meals was dismissed by most people who have heard stories of how it cannot cook food as well as a standard oven or if it could then their was no way that you should ever attempt to make desserts with one. The dessert would be raw in places or burnt. Both are false. You will be able to make fantastic desserts with your microwave. I am talking about cakes, cookies, pies and off the wall items such as Turkish delight and truffles..

A microwave oven has weaknesses, but desserts are not one of them. In this book you are going to find 25 world class recipes. You will discovery that the microwave can handle both sweet and savory dishes equally..

If you are ready let's makes a few desserts with Mic.

# Chapter Two
# Sponge Cake

*I wanted to buy a candle holder, but the store didn't have one. So I got a cake.* - Mitch Hedberg

I have been waiting to write this book until I was able to try every single recipe that would be included. That meant trying a few dozen desserts so I waited until the guilt free holiday season before I dug into them. The first recipe is going to be sponge cake. I picked it because I saw a world class chef attempt to win my favorite cooking show, Cutthroat Kitchen, with it. He did not win, but the cake looked great and I knew at that moment it was time to bless the world with a great microwave dessert cookbook. Okay, let's make sponge cake.

*Ingredients*
¼ cup sugar
½ cup flour
⅓ cup melted butter
1 teaspoon baking powder
1 egg
2 tablespoons milk

To cook this you are going to need a ramekin. This is a porcelain or plastic dish used for baking and serving. I like the plastic one better for this recipe. You are going to have enough batter for about two cakes. The mixing is easy. You are going to combine all of the ingredients into a bowl and blend with a hand mixer. Once the mix is smooth you are going to pour equal amounts into the two ramekins and then microwave. You are going to cook them for about 60 seconds in a 600 watt microwave oven. For every 100 watts above this you are going to remove a second of microwave cooking time. Too much time and the cake will be too flaky and too little time it will be too moist inside. When first attempting this recipe I suggest that you cook the ramekins separately so that you can see if the cooking time is correct.

Now remove from ramekin, if it sticks use a butter knife. Top with whip cream or icy and serve.

# Chapter Three
## Apple Cobbler

*"Cut my pie into four pieces, I don't think I could eat eight."* - Yogi Berra

Apple Cobbler is like a country way of saying pie. If you ate dessert on The Walton's you would not have pie you would have some of grandma's apple cobbler. I am sure that that pie would have been made in an old fashion oven, the kind that you put wood in or an early gas stove, but this one is going to be baked in your microwave oven.

*Ingredients*
5 cups of thinly sliced and peeled granny Smith apples
½ cup of sugar
2 tablespoons of flour or 1 tablespoon of cornstarch
½ teaspoon of cinnamon
*Topping ingredients*
¾ cups of biscuit mix
⅓ cup of milk
3 tablespoons of sugar
½ teaspoon of ground cinnamon

Now you are going to grab a 1 and ½ quart microwave dish. Next mix the flour, sugar and cinnamon. Sprinkle this over the apples and toss until coated. Cover dish and microwave on high for about 3 ½ minutes or until apples are tender.

In another bowl you are going to combine the biscuit mix, milk and 2 of the teaspoons of sugar. Now drop tablespoons full over the apples. Then you are going to mix the remaining sugar and cinnamon before sprinkling over the top of mixture. Now microwave for 5 - 6 minutes. Test with a fork, if it comes out clean then the cobbler is done and you are ready to eat.

# Chapter Four
## Pralines In A Microwave

*I was 32 when I started cooking; up until then, I just ate.* -Julia Child

*Ingredients*

  1 ½ cups of brown sugar
  ¼ teaspoon salt
  ⅔ heavy cream
  2 tablespoons margarine
  1 ½ cups pecan halves
  1 teaspoon vanilla extract

Grab your microwave bowl and in it we are going to mix the cream, sugar, margarine, salt and pecans. Cook this in the microwave for about nine minutes taking a break once to stir it. Allow to rest for a minute then add the vanilla and stir for two to three minutes more. Coat some wax paper with butter and drop teaspoonfuls of mixture onto the paper. When it has cool and set you are ready to eat.

# Chapter Five
# Super Easy Microwave Cornbread

Some of you may wish to argue as to whether or not cornbread is a desert or not. It is a bread and depending on what type of cornmeal is used to make the bread it is a sweetbread. It s normally used with gravy or butter, but taste great with all kinds of jams and jelly. I am including it in my little desert book because I tend to like it with jelly.

*Ingredients*
½ cup of flour
½ cup cornmeal
2 tablespoons white sugar
2 teaspoons of baking powder
½ teaspoon salt
½ cup milk
1 egg
2 tablespoons of vegetable oil

This is going to be super easy. You are going to grab a large microwave safe bowl and a hand mixer. You are going to put all of the ingredients in the bowl and mix until smooth.

Now we are going to place this in the microwave and cook on high for about three minutes. Test the center with a toothpick or fork. If it comes out clean the cornbread is done and if not hit it for another 30 seconds.

# Chapter Six
## Awesome Microwave Fudge

*"Happiness is a piece of fudge caught on the first bounce."* - Author: Charles M. Schulz

When I was a child I thought of fudge as being thick chocolate cake. This was one of the first dessert recipes that attempted with a microwave and is still one of my favorites.

*Ingredients*

½ cup unsweetened cocoa powder

4 cups of confectioners sugar

¼ cup milk

½ cup butter

2 teaspoons vanilla extract

Now we are going to grease a 9 x 9 microwave dish.

In a microwave bowl we are going to stir the sugar and cocoa powder. Then pour milk over this and drop butter into bowl. Do not mix yet. We are putting it into the microwave oven and heat for about a minute to a minute and a half or until butter is melted. Stir in the vanilla and mix by hand until mixture is rich and smooth. Now pour into the dish and place in the freezer for 10 minutes. The fudge should form up in the freezer and when you remove it the fudge should be firm enough to cut into squares and serve.

# Chapter Seven
# Baked Apples

Ingredients
- 2 apples
- 2 tablespoons brown sugar
- 1 teaspoon ground cinnamon
- 1 teaspoon ground nutmeg
- 2 teaspoons butter

First we are going to core the apples, leaving the bottoms intact.

Next in a bowl we are going to mix the cinnamon, sugar and nutmeg. Once mixed we are going to spoon this mix equally into each apple. Then we are going to top both apples with a teaspoon of butter. Now place them in a dish, top the dish and bake in the microwave for 3 ½ to 4 minutes and or until tender to the touch. Remove from oven and allow to cool for about 5 minutes before serving.

# Chapter Eight
## Amazing Microwave Chocolate Cake

*"Chemically speaking, chocolate really is the world's perfect food."* -
Michael Levine

One of the top three reasons that you picked up a dessert cookbook was to get to the chocolate cake. For some of us it is the reason we go to the supermarket and for others chocolate cake is the reason we get up in the morning. This recipe is the perfect excuse to make a chocolate cake. Do I have to say more?

*Ingredients*
¼ cup white sugar
3 tablespoons butter
1 egg
1 teaspoon vanilla extract
¼ cup milk
½ cup flour
2 tablespoons cocoa powder
¼ teaspoon baking powder
¼ teaspoon salt

Find a microwave safe bowl and spray it with nonstick spray before setting aside.

In a bowl we are going to mix the sugar, butter, egg, vanilla, and milk with a hand mixer. Now add the flour, cocoa, salt and baking powder. Mix until smooth before pouring into the bowl we have prepared.

Cover and cook for 2 to 2 ½ minutes. The cake is done when it springs back when pressed. Now allow the cake to cook for 5 to 10 minutes then turn the bowl upside on a plate to remove cake before serving.

# Chapter Nine
# Microwave Truffles

*Ingredients*
> ½ pound of semisweet chocolate
> ⅓ cup of toasted finely chopped pecans
> ¼ cup butter
> ¼ cup whipped cream
> ¼ teaspoon almond extract

You are going to get 24 paper foil mini muffin cups and place them on a baking sheet. Now carefully spoon in ½ teaspoon of the pecans into each cup. When finished you will set aside remaining pecans.

Now in a large microwave bowl we are going to mix the chocolate and butter. Next microwave this for 90 seconds to 2 minutes or until melted. Mix in the cream and extract with a hand mixer until well blended. Now pour equally into the cup and top them off with the remaining pecans. Next place them into the refrigerator until they set.

# Chapter Ten
# The World's Best Microwave Raisin Bread Pudding

I use to love raisin bread when I was a kid. I would run through the supermarket, find it and run back with it to hand off to my mother who would mostly tell me to put it back, but there were times that she wouldn't and I would get it home where I would pick the raisins off and eat the cinnamon frosting from the bread ends. That is probably the reason why I went through a few loaves of raisin bread before I was able to hang on to enough slices to make this recipe.

*Ingredients*
16 slices of raisin bread, cut and cubed
½ cup of sugar
A dash of cinnamon
2 cups of milk
¼ cup butter
5 beaten eggs
½ cup white sugar
1 teaspoon vanilla extract

Line a 2 quart baking dish with the raisin bread. Next sprinkle the sugar and cinnamon evenly over this before setting it aside.

Now we are going to place the milk and the butter in a glass bowl and cooking the microwave for 5 minutes on medium. Remove from microwave oven and quickly stir in the sugar, vanilla and egg. You will want to stir quickly because if you do not then the hot milk may cook the beaten eggs before they are mixed in. Now pour this over the cubed bread. Cover with plastic wrap and cook at a medium heat in the microwave for about 18 minutes or until pudding has set.

# Chapter Eleven
# Cherry Crisp

*I cook, I create, I'm incredibly excited by what I do, I've still got a lot to achieve.* - Gordon Ramsay

*Ingredients*

¼ cup butter

⅓ cup flour

1 (20-21 ounce) can of cherry pie filling

¾ cups brown sugar

⅔ cup quick oats

Grab a 9 inch microwave pie pan and carefully spoon the filling into the pan making sure that it is evenly placed. Now in a bowl we are going to mix the sugar, oats and flour. Now add in the butter and mix until it looks like a crumble. Sprinkle over the filling and microwave on high for about 14 minutes.

You should serve this warm and maybe with the flavor of ice cream that you like best.

# Chapter Twelve
## Peanut Brittle

As a kid use to love peanut brittle. I loved it because it could sit there for weeks and it never went bad. I would find the stuff in drawers or in jacket pockets. Little bits of tooth damaging goodness. You are probably thinking back to the last time that you ate peanut brittle and cannot wait to do again.

*Ingredients*
2 cups white sugar
1 cup light corn syrup
⅔ cup of peanuts
2 tablespoons butter
2 teaspoons baking soda
2 teaspoons vanilla extract

In a large casserole dish we are going to mix the sugar, corn syrup and peanuts. Next microwave on high for 12 full minutes. Then stir in the butter and vanilla, cook on high for 4 minutes. Now mix in the baking soda.

Now quickly butter a cookie sheet and pour the mix on it to cool. When it has cool you can break it into tasty brittle sized pieces.

# Chapter Thirteen
# Chocolate Pie

*Ingredients*
   1 (9 inch) pie shell
   ¾ cup white sugar
   ¼ cup cornstarch
   ⅓ cup cocoa powder
   ¼ teaspoon salt
   2 cups milk
   3 beaten egg yolks
   2 softened tablespoons of butter
   1 teaspoon vanilla extract
*Meringue Ingredients*
   3 egg whites, beaten
   ¼ teaspoon cream of tartar
   6 tablespoons of white sugar
   ½ teaspoon vanilla extract

First preheat the oven to 375 degrees F or 190 degrees C. Yes, I know. I said oven. We need both a standard oven and a microwave to make this recipe.

In a casserole dish we are going to mix the sugar, cornstarch, cocoa, salt and ½ cup of milk. Once it has mixed well you can stir in the remaining milk. Now microwave on high for 6 to 8 minutes. Stir once while it is cooking and remove with it has thickened.

Now in a bowl you will pour a small amount of the mixture that you have removed from microwave. You will grab a hand mixer and blend the egg yolks into the bowl. Now you will pour this back into the warm mixture and microwave on high for about 90 seconds. Remove from microwave and now blend in the butter and vanilla until smooth. Next you are going to pour this into the pie shell.

Next we are going to make the meringue. Pour the egg whites and cream of tartar into the bowl and grab your hand mixer. Set the mixer on high and beat this until foamy. Now slowly pour in two tablespoons at a time of the sugar until stiff peaks form. Now add in the vanilla.

Now spread the meringue over the pie filling. Seal the rim of pie with aluminum foil, place in oven and bake for 7-8 minutes or until meringue is turning brown.

# Chapter Fourteen
## Microwave Flan

*Ingredients*

Divide 3 cups of sugar
2 cups milk
1 tablespoon vanilla
4 eggs

Grab a saucepan and over a medium heat we are going to heat one cup of the sugar. Do not stir the dry sugar until you see it start to bubble and melt. When the sugar is melted and is a golden brown remove it from the heat and pour it into a 9 inch ceramic pie plate. Making sure that the bottom is evenly coated.

Next in a bowl we are going to mix the milk,vanilla, remaining sugar and eggs. You can do this with a hand mixer or by hand. Now pour onto the pie plate.

Place in microwave and cook at half power for 7 minutes. Now turn it up to full and cook for another 8 minutes. Stick a fork in the middle if it comes out clean the flan is done if not then cook another minute repeat fork test and do this over and over until fork comes out clean. Now pop it in the refrigerator and cook for a while before serving.

# Chapter Fifteen
# They Call it Mud Cake In Mississippi

The coolest thing about this recipe is that most of you do not have a clue what Mississippi mud cake is. Well you are going to have to cook it to find out. All I can say is that if you love desserts you are going to love this one.

*Ingredients*

1 cup margarine

4 eggs

¼ cup unsweetened cocoa powder

2 cups white sugar

1 ½ cups flour

1 cup chopped walnuts

1 teaspoon vanilla extract

2 cups miniature marshmallows

4 cups confectioners sugar

⅓ cup unsweetened cocoa powder

⅔ cups milk

Grab a 9 x 13 microwave safe cake dish. Now we are going to melt the margarine, this should take about thirty seconds and then mix in the cocoa and stir in the eggs. Mix well before adding in the 2 cups of sugar, flour, nuts and vanilla. Once mix looks smooth you will make in the microwave on high for about 11 minutes. Remove from microwave and cover with the marshmallows.

Time to make frosting. In a microwave safe bowl mix the confectioners sugar, cocoa and milk. Cook in the microwave for about 2 minutes. Stir it and pour over the cake before it cools.

# Chapter Sixteen
## The Awesome Chocolate chip Cookie Mug

*I cook, I create, I'm incredibly excited by what I do, I've still got a lot to achieve.* -Gordon Ramsay

Chocolate chip cookies are heaven on earth when done well. I think about my little girl every time I sneak off and make this recipe for myself. You see if she knew that there was a chocolate chip cookie in my boring looking mug she would hit me with her teddy bear, (the one with batteries in it) and run off with my cookie mug. What I am saying is that this cookie is for the selfish. Do not feel guilty it is okay to be selfish where cookies are concerned. Santa Claus is, think about it. Has Santa ever shared his cookies with you. He shows up, eats his cookies, drinks his milk and he is gone, leaving a crumb that is too small for a mouse; or is that the Grinch?

*Ingredients*
1 tablespoon firm brown sugar
1 tablespoon butter
½ teaspoon vanilla extract
¼ teaspoon salt
1 egg yolk
1 tablespoon chocolate chips
3 tablespoons flour

Now we are going to grab a mug, drop the butter in and hit it for about thirty seconds in the oven. Next grab a fork and mix in the sugar, salt and vanilla. Then add the egg yolk until well mixed before mixing in the flour. Now we are going to add the chocolate chips last and mix then it. Place in oven and bake on high for 45 to 55 seconds.

Understand that it may not look fully cooked when you remove from oven, do not worry. Give it a minute or two to cook and dig in. For more cookies just grab more mugs and repeat the recipe.

# Chapter Seventeen
# Turkish Delight

This recipe can make 50 to 60 pieces of candy. I believe that when people talk about this book it will be concerning this recipe. You are going to have to set it aside for a day so that the candy can set properly. This European candy made famous to most of us through the books or films The Lion, The Witch and the Wardrobe was something that I had not tried until this recipe came along. One word on mixing this recipe, I would a whisk rather than a hand mixer.

*Ingredients*
3 cups sugar
2 ½ cups of cold water
¾ cup cornstarch,
½ cup of cornstarch to dust the candies when cooked
¼ cup light corn syrup
1 tablespoon lemon extract
2 drops of red food coloring
½ cup powdered sugar
Cooking spray for pan

Pour the water into a one gallon glass bowl. Mix in ¾ cup of cornstarch until dissolved. Microwave 2 minutes, remove from oven, give it a quick mixing and return to oven to cook for another

3 minute or until the mixture begins to whiten. Remove and mix some more until it begins to look and move like paste. Now add sugar corn syrup. Heat in microwave for another five minutes. Remove from oven, mix until mixture smooth and cook for another 5 minutes before stirring in the lemon juice and food coloring.

You are going to mix this until the color is even. Return to oven and cook for 3 more minutes.

At this point the mixture sure be very thick and hard to mix further. At this point you can allow it to cool. After it has cooled you should be able to pick it up and roll it into balls without it being tacky to the touch.

Now grease a 8 x 8 loaf pan with cooking spray and pour in the candy mixture. Spread evenly and allow candy to set for a few hours at room temperature. Next we are going to grab a knife and cut the candy into even squares.

In a bowl mix the remaining cornstarch and powdered sugar. Take the cut candy squares and roll them in this mix. At this point the candy is ready to serve. You can eat it as it or pierce with toothpicks or Popsicle sticks and top them with sprinkles or crushed nuts.

# Chapter Eighteen
# Microwave Peach Cobbler In A Mug

*Ingredients*
- 1 Tablespoon butter
- 2 ½ tablespoon of milk
- 3 ½ tablespoons of white cake mix
- ¼ teaspoon of cinnamon
- 4 - 5 ounces of diced or sliced peaches in syrup

First we are going to put the butter in the mug and place it in the microwave for 30 seconds to melt. In a bowl we are going to mix together cinnamon and cake mix and milk. Mix well before pouring into mug over the butter. Allow to rest on top of butter without stirring. Drain about half the liquid from the peaches, discard, and pour the peaches and remaining syrup on top of mix. Set the microwave at half power and cook this for about 3 ½ minutes to 4 minutes. Remove and allow to cool for a few minutes until cool enough to eat. If you cannot wait you can top with a scoop of ice cream.

# Chapter Nineteen
## Caramel Popcorn

*Ingredients*
10 - 12 ounces of popped popcorn
1 cup brown sugar
½ cup margarine or butter
¼ cup light corn syrup
½ teaspoon salt
1 teaspoon vanilla extract
½ teaspoon baking soda

Pour the popcorn into large brown paper bag and set it aside for later.

In a casserole dish mix the brown sugar, margarine, corn syrup, vanilla and salt. Heat this in the microwave for 3 minutes, remove and stir for half a minute before returning to microwave and cooking for another 90 seconds. Remove and stir in the baking soda.

Now we are going to pour this mix into the popcorn filled paper bag, roll the top closed and shake it for about a minute to coat the popcorn well. Next put back into the microwave and cook for 1 more minute. Tear open bag and allow to cool before storing in a plastic airtight container.

# Chapter Twenty
## Maple Fudge

*Ingredients*
  1 pound (16 ounces) confectioners sugar
  3 tablespoons milk
  1 tablespoon butter
  ¾ cup chopped walnuts
  We are going to line a microwave dish with plastic wrap.

  Next we will pour the sugar into a bowl, add in the milk, butter and maple extract. Do not mix or stir. Heat the bowl in the microwave for 3 minutes. Remove from oven and stir in the walnuts. Stir until the fudge begins to form. Next pour into the lined dish, smooth it out and place in the refrigerator until it gets firm. Remove the fudge from pan by using the plastic to lift and place on a cutting board and cut into small squares before placing in a container for storage.

# Chapter Twenty One
# Oreo Cookie Creamy Fudge

Think about it. Oreo cookies and fudge. Fudge and Oreo cookies. Do I have to sell that concept to you? Have you ever eaten Oreo cookies and or fudge? Well if you have then I have some really good news for you. They taste great together. .

*Ingredients*

12 - 14 oreos broken into tiny pieces

1 can of condensed milk

3 cups of white chocolate chips

First we are going to line the bottom of a baking dish with parchment paper. While in a bowl we are going to combine the milk and chocolate chips. Stir them and then place in microwave for 30 - 40 seconds or until chocolate is melted.

Now spread half of the oreos over the bottom of the pan. Pour the white chocolate over it and coat with remaining oreo cookie bits. Now press the cookie bits into the chocolate. Place pan into refrigerator for 4 to 6 hours. When it has set you may cut it into squares with a knife and serve.

# Chapter Twenty Two
# Cheesecake in the Microwave

*I might put a nicer pair of heels on and a cooler outfit, but I'm still that naughty girl who likes a slice of cheesecake on my day off.* - Jessie J

*Ingredients*
   1 egg
   2 ounces of cream cheese
   2 tablespoons of sour cream
   ½ teaspoon lemon juice or extract
   ¼ teaspoon vanilla extract
   3 -4 tablespoons sugar

This is going to be super easy. Mix all of the ingredients on a microwave safe bowl. You can use a fork or whisk. Now place the bowl in the microwave and heat for 30 seconds, stir and repeat two times more for a total of 90 seconds. Now you can remove it from the bowl, place in a mug and refrigerate for at least an hour before serving. Feel free to top this with whipped cream or fresh fruit.

# Chapter Twenty Three
## Berry Coffee Cake In a Microwave

*Cook ingredients that you are used to cooking by other techniques, such as fish, chicken, or hamburgers. In other words be comfortable with the ingredients you are using.* - Bobby Flay

*Ingredients*

½ teaspoon sugar
½ tablespoon butter
1 tablespoon brown rice syrup
2 tablespoons applesauce
½ teaspoon vanilla extract
¼ cup flour
¼ teaspoon baking powder
dash of salt
2 tablespoons of berries

*Streusel topping:*

1 tablespoon butter
1 tablespoon flour
1 tablespoon brown sugar
¼ teaspoon cinnamon

Now we will grab a mug and drop the butter in it. We are going to place it in the microwave oven to melt for about ten seconds. Now mix in the rice syrup and brown sugar. applesauce, baking powder and salt. Stir with fork until mixed well. Add the berry of your choice and mix in gently.

Next in a bowl you are going to mix all of the ingredients for the streusel topping. You want it to feel to the touch like grains of sand with small pebbles mixed in. Now you will top the mix in the mug with this and place in microwave. Cook for 75 - 85 seconds. Now grab your spoon and have a taste.

# Chapter Twenty Four
## Banana Microwave Cake

*Ingredients*
- 1 teaspoon cinnamon
- ⅓ cup finely chopped walnuts
- ¼ cup brown sugar
- ¾ cup all purpose flour
- 1 teaspoon baking soda
- ½ teaspoon salt
- ⅔ cup shortening or margarine
- ½ cup brown sugar
- 2 medium eggs
- 1 teaspoon vanilla extract
- 1 cup of mashed bananas
- ⅓ cup milk

We are going to mix ¼ cup of brown sugar with walnuts and cinnamon. Mix well in a small bowl before setting aside. In a second bowl we are going to blend the salt, wheat flour, flour and baking soda.

Now grab a and mixer and mix together the shortening, and ½ cup brown sugar. add in the eggs and vanilla before blending in the bananas. Now dump in the flour mix and then the milk. When mixture is smooth you will greasy a glass baking dish and spread the batter evenly. Then you will top with the walnuts.

Next we are going to microwave at medium for about ten minutes. Remove from microwave oven and place it in a standard or toaster oven set at about 250 for 6 to 10 minutes longer. If you do not have a toaster or standard oven then you can finish it in the microwave by setting oven to its lowest setting and cooking for another 5 to 7 minutes.

Remove from oven, cool at room temperature for a few minutes before serving.

# Chapter Twenty Five
## Microwave S'mores

*You learn to cook so that you don't have to be a slave to recipes. You get what's in season and you know what to do with it.* - Julia Child

*Ingredients*

¼ cup flour

2 tablespoons cocoa powder

2 tablespoons sugar

¼ teaspoon salt

2 tablespoon vegetable oil

2 tablespoon water

2 tablespoon marshmallows

1 graham crushed cracker

1 mini Hershey's chocolate candy bar

Now we are going to grab a large mug and in it you are going to mix with a fork the cocoa powder, sugar, flour and salt. Then add the water and vegetable oil. When it appears smooth you can mix a tablespoon of your mini marshmallows. Now break half the Hershey's candy bar into bits and press them into the batter. Top with the graham crackers and microwave on medium for 30 seconds.

Put the rest of the marshmallows on top and remaining candy bar in bits. Place back in oven for 20 to 30 seconds more and remove when chocolate is melted. The S'mores are done and you are ready to eat.

# Don't miss out!

Click the button below and you can sign up to receive emails whenever rodney cannon publishes a new book. There's no charge and no obligation.

**Sign Me Up!**

https://books2read.com/r/B-A-YPE-ILJN

Connecting independent readers to independent writers.

Printed in Great Britain
by Amazon